A Butterfly's Voice

A Novella

Faleeha Hassan

inner child press, ltd.

Credits

Author

Faleeha Hassan

Translator

William Hutchins

Editor

hülya n. yılmaz, Ph.D.

Cover Design

William S. Peters Sr.

&

inner child press, ltd.

General Information

A Butterfly's Voice

Author: Faleeha Hassan

1st Edition: 2020

Publisher Information:
Inner Child Press
intouch@innerchildpress.com
www.innerchildpress.com

ISBN-13: 978-1-952081-07-1 (inner child press, ltd.)

$ 12.99

Table of Contents

Epilogue

A Butterfly's Voice

A Novella

Faleeha Hassan

Chapter

1

A Butterfly's Voice

Even the consulting physicians were puzzled when I lost my voice.

The year 1979 doesn't just preoccupy me; that's when the darkness began.

We were invited to a wedding in the desert, the Iraqi desert. Most of the young men there were dancing the *dabke*[1]. A few others were helping women prepare food.

My father sat in a large tent with the older men. They were nervously discussing the new president, who had assumed power after serving as vice-president in the previous government.

When an elderly *shaykh*[2] observed: "They say he's a thug," everyone turned toward him with surprise.

"Isn't the weather great!" Salih's father exclaimed to change the subject, away from the new president, who had only been in power for a few days. "It's good we decided to have Salih's wedding at this time of the year!" Some men quickly expressed their agreement and began discussing the noble bride, who was of impeccable lineage and from a fine family. I smiled broadly when I saw my mother, who was seated in another tent across the way, move her shoulders and mimic the gestures of the young men dancing the *dabke*. As I tried to slip away from the tent where I sat with my father and the other men, he looked at me and said, "Don't stray too far. Their dogs are aggressive!"

"Let her go to her mother in the other tent," a man suggested. "She's a big girl. Nowadays girls like her are married!"

I ran quickly to the women's tent, almost dying from embarrassment after hearing this. I pressed up against my

---

[1] Dabke: A folk-dance native to ethnic groups in Levant and performed widely at weddings and similar joyous occasions by the people of Lebanon, Jordan, Syria, Palestine, and Iraq.

[2] Shaykh: An Arab leader; a male member of a ruling Arab family, in a Muslim community or organization

grandmother, surveying the faces of married women and trying to guess their ages.

The wedding festivities lasted three days. Then, we returned to our city, but that old man's words echoed in my ears whenever I saw a picture of the new president, who looked younger and more handsome than his predecessor.

"Thug" – my father declined to clarify this word's meaning when I asked. Instead, he changed the subject and said: "You're young. Over the course of time, you'll learn what words mean."

My grandmother said, "A thug is someone who kills even the members of his own family." My mother added, "A thug is a person who kills people for no reason at all."

I couldn't imagine that such a handsome, youthful face masked a thug. In the movies tough, such men as described by my grandmother and mother now were scary and ugly. They usually had yellow teeth.

I didn't grasp the full meaning of this word till 1980, when conditions changed. Many of the trees that had formed a green belt around my city – Najaf – were cut down. The sky turned dark and lost its blue color. As for clouds . . . well, we didn't know where they had gone. The water-level in the rivers gradually dropped till they almost ran dry. Spring and autumn ceased to exist. Our only seasons were a bitterly cold winter and an arid and insufferably hot summer.

Dust and sand storms did not wait for any season. They were constant visitors that robbed all colors of their splendor, reducing them to a dusty gray. I never heard anything more about that old fellow, but all the men in my city began to embrace his hatred for our new president.

My father, who worked as a school janitor, had earned only a primary school certificate. My mother had learned to recite the *Quran*[3] by heart, but that was the extent of her education. My family consisted of me, my father, mother, grandmother, and

---

[3] Quran: The sacred book of the religion of Islam

younger brother Salam. We didn't own a house. We lived in a lengthy succession of rental homes. Most of these were in Najaf's Khan al-Makhdar area, which was bisected by a large public market, frequented by shoppers from all regions of the city. In fact, you encountered Bedouin Arabs, Persians, and Afghans there as well.

On the first day of my summer vacation, I was practicing my hobby of drawing pencil portraits of people I loved. I told myself that the art teacher would surely give me high marks once I completed this portrait of my grandmother and submitted it to her during the next school year.

However, I felt scared and stopped drawing when I remembered what my religion teacher had said after she happened to see one of my drawings: "You know that on Judgment Day, God will ask you to breathe life into this portrait. When you fail, He will punish you by casting you into the deepest pit of hell's fire, because you tried to imitate Him through one of His creations."

Just to be sure, I asked my Arabic language teacher, "Is drawing forbidden?" Perhaps, the religion teacher was wrong.

She replied, "Yes." Then she added, "Our wonderful Prophet, Muhammad, may God bless him and grant him peace, said: 'Those most severely punished on Judgment Day will be the portraitists, who imitate God's creative power.' (So said the truthful Messenger of God.) 'Imitators' are hideous infidels."

"Why," I asked, "does God give us the ability to draw and then punish us when we make pictures?"

She recoiled and looked away. From that day forward, she never gave me full marks on any Arabic language exam, even if I answered all the questions correctly.

So, I tore up the portrait of my grandmother, not knowing what to think. Then, I went to look for something else to do with my free time.

My father returned at noon, and we sat down to eat lunch. As usual, he placed my little brother, Salam, on his lap and began to feed him one morsel after another. What was unusual was that he didn't smile at Salam or chat with us, as he always did. He seemed tense. My mother refrained from looking at him but told him in a hushed voice that our neighbor Abu Mahdi had come and asked for him. My father placed Salam back on the floor and stood up. My mother rose as well and said, "There's nothing we can do. This is God's decree!"

My grandmother commented furiously, "It is not God's decree. It's his! I don't know what people will do. Where will they go to escape from him? Damn him."

Hearing her, my father returned quickly and whispered, "Mother, I beg you: Don't raise your voice. Someone may hear you."

As he headed to his room, tears began to flow from his eyes. I was startled to see my father cry. This was the first time I had seen him weep. What was happening?

We didn't finish our meal that day, and the plates remained where they were on the mat. When my mother returned, she cleared them away, carrying them back to the kitchen. I tried to hear as much as I could of what my grandmother was saying after she entered my father's room and closed the door behind her. I could not hear complete, comprehensible sentences. All I could make out were a few words like "deportation" and names like Furhud and Abu Mahdi.

"Mama, what's happening?" I asked after I hurried to pick up a plate and take it to the kitchen.

"Nothing, Dear. Nothing. These matters don't concern you. Why you didn't eat anything! There's *ka'ak*[4] to dunk if you're hungry. I'll make tea for everyone." She came back to feed my brother rice mixed with bean broth, but curiosity was almost killing me. If these matters didn't concern me, why had our house gone into mourning now? What was happening?"

Alarmed, I jumped when I heard relentless knocking on the door. All the same, I rushed at once to open it. Our neighbor

---

[4] Ka'ak: A type of savory doughnut

Abu Mahdi stood there. He smiled and asked, "How are you, dear Nasura[5]?"

"Fine. Praise God. How are you, Uncle?"

"Praise God. Is Papa here?"

"Yes, he is, Uncle. Just a moment. Mama, Uncle Mahdi's at the door."

"Ask him to step inside, Dear," she replied as she entered my father's room to tell him. Father hurried out and pressed Abu Mahdi to his bosom, hugging him hard while both men sobbed.

Their sobs proved contagious. Yes, everyone started crying – even my little brother and my mother who was in the bedroom. I wept too, not knowing why.

I never saw Abu Mahdi again, and his house remained locked. No one moved in; at least not at first.

Before he left for work the next day, my father advised my mother and grandmother: "If you go to the market and see goods that belonged to the deportees – don't buy any."

My mother replied, "Yes, I most certainly won't!"

That morning, my grandmother sank into a profound silence that I wasn't able to penetrate or even to sense its depth, no matter how hard I tried. So, I decided I had to figure out what was happening. I told my mother I wanted to go to the market with her, and she actually took me. We walked side by side as each of us tried to check out the scene with fleeting glances, our ears alert for the calls of vendors hawking their piles of goods. We lowered our gaze to avoid faces that looked both angry and scared. The market seemed a cresting river that swallowed all shoppers, leaving only the piles of goods visible.

I saw displays of entire households offered at really cheap prices: stuff like washing machines, fridges, gas and kerosene cookers, table lamps of various sizes, designs, and colors, chairs, tables, water heaters, as well as electric, gas, and kerosene stoves. Yes, even whole sets of household furnishings were on sale. Some folks were bargaining for rock bottom

---

[5] "Nasura" is the nickname in Iraq for "Intisar".

prices. Others purchased things they didn't need, merely to buy something. People like my mother walked by these displays without asking about the prices, because they were sure the items were being sold under duress.

The market's clamor continued unabated for more than a week. Most of these vendors were men. Women sold their belongings in a different way. They knocked on doors at noon and offered items small enough to carry. These were mostly valuable personal items like men's and women's wristwatches, used clothing that looked as good as new, cosmetic cases, bars of scented soap, bracelets, and silver jewelry goldsmiths wouldn't buy.

Whenever one of these women knocked on our door, my mother would apologize: "Abu Salam made me promise not to buy anything. Forgive me." Then, the woman would sadly leave our door.

Before my grandmother's friend Hajja Umm Siham left – some said for Iran, where her father's relatives lived, while others said for Turkey, where her mother's relatives were – she offered my grandmother a choice of either a new piece of cloth from which Hajja Umm Siham would make her a blouse or a silk shawl, which had the *Du'a'a al-Jawshan al-Kabir*[6] written on it with saffron; on the understanding that Hajja Umm Siham would fashion a shroud for her from it. My grandmother chose the shawl and instructed us, in her friend's presence, to bury her in this shawl for two reasons. First of all, the fabric came from the land of the Prophet Muhammad (PBUH), Muslims' guide, who would plead for her with God on Judgment Day. Secondly, it would serve as a memento of the two women's friendship, which had endured for many years, even though they came from different backgrounds.

Once Abu Mahdi's household and Hajja Umm Siham departed, no one visited us anymore, and our house, which now

---

[6] Du'a'a al-Jawshan al-Kabir: A lengthy prayer the Angel Gabriel is said to have taught the Prophet Muhammad to use like a body armor

stood between two vacant houses, was isolated. My father's expression was always sad, and my grandmother spent all her time with me. So, she began telling me stories of her childhood, her girlfriends, her marriage to my grandfather, and even about spring, a season that we no longer experienced in this city.

My mother was the only family member to occupy herself primarily with my younger brother, who had begun to crawl. She seemed the happiest family member. Once my brother fell asleep, she practiced her one hobby, which was crocheting.

For my part, I wasn't allowed to leave the house alone, because I was no longer considered a child, as my father pointed out. When I passed the elementary school certificate exam, before the new school year began, a black *abaya*[7] was made for me. I had to wear it whenever I left the house, no matter how near my destination was.

The middle school wasn't far from our house. In fact, it was located at the end of the market. A large sign over its doorway read: "Algeria." I practiced wearing the abaya at home and almost fell repeatedly because it was so long. Then, my grandmother hemmed it to match my height. My father bought a dark blue polyester fabric and white cloth to be sewn into a smock and a blouse, respectively, as a uniform for my new school. My mother purchased white shoes with white laces for me too. When my grandmother went to the city's controller's office to collect payment from my grandfather's pension, as she did every month, she took me with her. We visited the tomb of *Imam*[8] Ali (PUH) and then went to the great *suq* – the covered market where shops sell gold jewelry, textiles, shoes, watches, silver, abayas, whistles, cooking oil, pickles, and so on.

"What do you think about these shoes," Grandmother asked me.

"I'm crazy about them. I loved them at first sight."

---

[7] Abaya: A robe-like dress that women in some Islamic countries wear
[8] Imam: The person who leads prayers in a mosque.

She turned to the shopkeeper and, pointing to me, asked, "Do you have these in her size?"

"Aunt, please step inside," he responded. I followed her inside and sat down to try on the shoes, enjoying something I had never experienced before.

All the shoes I had ever worn had been chosen for me by my father or mother. I was content with them, because I had no alternative. Neither one of my parents would ask me before buying them. They would simply tell me: "These are great!" or "They're lovely!" or "They look splendid on you!" This was the first time I ever sat down to try on new shoes that I had picked out.

The man brought the shoes, which he placed on a clean cloth spread on the floor beneath my feet, for me to try on. Closing my eyes, I imagined I was Cinderella – the beautiful girl I had seen on TV.

"What do you think of them?" Grandmother asked.

"They're nice."

"Just nice? Does that mean you don't really like them?"

Pointing to another pair of shoes with high heels, I said, "I want those."

The shopkeeper objected: "You can't wear those to school."

"But they're really beautiful. I like them a lot," I replied.

"No problem. Fetch those too. We'll take both pairs. Nasura graduated first in her class and deserves to have both pairs," Grandmother told him.

The man placed each pair of the shoes in a pasteboard box, after checking the sizes, and put both boxes in a plastic bag, which he handed to me. I was so delighted at being able to wear two pairs of the most beautiful shoes that my heart beat faster.

My grandmother handed the shopkeeper the money, and we left. I was blissfully happy and wished then I had a girlfriend to tell about my new shoes, which I had picked out myself for the very first time in my life. Grandmother asked if I wanted to buy anything else, but I thanked her and said no.

My delight with those shoes rendered any desire to purchase something else superfluous. Before returning home, we stopped at a drugstore to buy her usual medicines for diabetes, high blood pressure, and gall bladder.

After the deportation of "undocumented aliens," the semi-deserted streets were frightening, and rumors spread that ghosts inhabited their empty houses. My father spent less time in the coffeehouse, and my family's main preoccupation was watching the news on TV.

Pictures of the President appeared in homes, schools, and the markets as well as on walls along the streets to an alarming degree. Even our house had a picture of him, smiling. My father hung it in the parlor so that any guest who visited us would see it.

In the other rooms of our house, we displayed pictures of imams, but in the room I shared with my grandmother, we had a black-and-white photo of my grandfather beside the imams' portraits.

A Butterfly's Voice

Chapter

2

A Butterfly's Voice

At four p.m. one Thursday, the padlock on the door of Abu Mahdi's house was broken, and a tall, burly man entered the house, inspected it, and emerged smiling.

At seven that evening, the same man returned with three women. They entered the house, cleaned it, and then left.

Friday morning, a large family we had never seen before moved into Abu Mahdi's house. No one in my family tried to make their acquaintance.

Their daily clamor persisted late into the night. So, we started to take the small television, which my father had recently purchased, to the roof terrace and slept there.

An entire month passed while we followed this practice, which my mother had suggested as a way of escaping from the voices of the children and women, who fought each other for the most trivial reasons.

Every day my father began bringing home a watermelon he split in half with a knife and placed on a platter. We wouldn't start eating it till seven or eight p.m. when the gentle breeze on the roof had cooled it.

Our house's large door didn't match the small size of the building, which had two rooms with a cramped, rectangular courtyard between them. The stairs to the roof were located in the courtyard, and the shower and toilet were beneath them.

That huge, gray door was set in a high wall slightly taller than the adjoining walls. Two large stone benches were located in front of this wall. My grandmother had often sat there chatting with her friend Hajja Umm Siham in the afternoon. They would talk nonstop till the muezzin issued the call to prayer from the tall, blue minaret of the mosque located in the center of the district.

I would sit behind the door to listen to their conversations, which transported me to truly amazing worlds. When they heard the call to prayer, each woman would return to her house to prepare to pray – already looking forward to meeting again the following afternoon.

This practice, which I had monitored since I was virtually an infant, continued till Hajja Umm Siham left for a place unknown – at least I had no idea where she had gone. I did not dare ask my grandmother for fear of upsetting her, since she did her best to hide her sorrow from me.

Our door closed for the sunset prayer. My mother and grandmother would pray in their respective bedrooms while I watched my little brother crawl and play. My father prayed with his friend in the district's mosque; then they would head to the coffeehouse.

Salam was my parents' prime source of delight. Had it not been for him, I think my mother wouldn't ever have smiled. I never felt jealous of him. Instead, I treated him like a living doll I very much loved.

I had heard my mother tell my grandmother how many female physicians she had consulted and how many pills she had swallowed before she became pregnant with him.

For this reason, he was much younger than me. I was twelve now, and he was just one and had only begun to crawl.

My father thought that Salam wouldn't develop into a healthy child, because he was small and feeble, but my grandmother believed that he was a normal child. Just because he was slow learning to crawl or walk, that didn't mean he was sick or developmentally challenged.

Now the door remained closed all day long; my grandmother hadn't sat on its step outside since her friend disappeared. When we heard knocking on the door, my mother would hurriedly pick up Salam, as if to protect him from an intruder.

The Muslim month containing Ashura, when all our streets were decked with black, had yet to arrive with its special rituals. Black pieces of cloth were hung on the walls of houses beside the prominent imams' portraits, which were decorated with green. Torches lit the evening, as many men and boys carried them along the streets. The sound of Shi'i dirges swelled from cassette players till they drowned out even the call to prayer.

I felt certain that month hadn't begun yet, even though I saw one of those large black cauldrons typical of this month. It was near our house, almost at our doorstep, and there was another one near our neighbor Abu Mahdi's house – I mean the house where Abu Mahdi used to live; a stranger lived there now.

I saw the two cauldrons when I opened the door for a woman who wanted to borrow a large knife. I raced to my mother to tell her what that woman had said. She replied indifferently, "Give the lady the knife and then quickly close the door." After doing that, I returned to my grandmother. Standing near her, I asked, "Granny, is it Ashura yet?"

"No, why do you ask?" She was counting her small, black prayer beads.

"I saw Ashura cauldrons by the door!"

My grandmother smiled, stopped praising God, and gently pulled me to her. She explained, "There aren't special pots only for Ashura."

I retorted: "Yes, there are large black pots for cooking *qima*[9] and rice."

She smiled again and said, "These large black pots are used to cook stews and rice for different events – not just for Ashura. When people celebrate a marriage or circumcision, any festive event that many people attend, large cauldrons are used to cook food for large banquets. Where did you see cauldrons today?"

"I saw two between our house and the new neighbors' house when I opened the door to hand the woman the knife she asked to borrow. So, I thought the month of Muharram must have begun."

"Ah, our new neighbor is probably hosting a party unrelated to Muharram." Then, she whispered: "Listen, Nasura, if any of them knocks on the door at sunset, don't open it. One of the new neighbors' kids might bring us some food. But we don't want to eat the food of those people who live in a house that doesn't belong to them. My dear Nasura, the people living

---

[9] Qima: Chopped or ground meat stewed with chickpeas

next door to us now are bad news. Whatever they do is sinful. God won't accept it. Even their prayers and fasting are sinful. If they have a girl your age in your school, or even in your class, don't make friends with her. I mean: don't talk to her much. She lives in a plundered house."

I quickly asked, "What's 'a plundered house,' Granny?"

"Listen: that house belongs to Abu Mahdi. The people living there now didn't buy or rent it from him, and that's a sin!"

"But, Granny, perhaps they're poor and don't have enough money to pay rent."

"That's no excuse! We're poor too. Don't you see how your father exhausts himself and suffers at work so we can rent the house we live in? We haven't thought even for a minute about living in a house without paying the owner some rent money for it. What would you think if we lived in a house we didn't own or pay rent for? Even if you accepted that, God wouldn't. He wouldn't accept any of your deeds, not even the good ones. In God's eyes and those of good people, you would be a thief."

"Does this mean our neighbors are crooks?"

"Yes, they are! In the eyes of both God and devout Muslims."

When I left my grandmother's room, I felt fearful. We were living next to thieves now! I would never open the door again, no matter how loudly they knocked. Then, I reflected I was being a ninny, because a thief doesn't knock on the door. He doesn't come to steal during daylight hours. *I'm a big girl now and must be brave. Yes, I won't accept any food from our neighbors, even if they offer me some, and I won't speak to their daughter in school if she tries to chat – assuming they have a girl in my school.*

My father knocked on the door, and I smiled when I let him in. He smiled too and said, "Princess, you grow prettier by the hour."

My father complimented me every day when I opened the door for him as a reward for performing this daily task.

Before I let him in, I would try to anticipate which compliment he would use. I succeeded sometimes; sometimes I didn't.

After my father came home that day, I didn't close the door immediately the way I usually do. Instead, I stood there, staring at the two cauldrons, each of which sat over an iron grill resting on tripods beneath which logs and embers blazed.

The two men who stood by the huge pots, busy cooking, had returned my father's greeting quickly. One stirred the chickpea and meat stew with a large ladle while the other man fed wood to the fire beneath the second pot, in which water was boiling furiously.

The sight of the red coals, rising flames, and the smell of the burning wood, combined with the stifling summer heat, made me stop and stare. The image of those two men corresponded to the portrayal of hell stored away in my head, based on my grandmother's descriptions of the inferno: a huge cauldron boiling ferociously, flaming wood and embers, and agents of divine justice preparing to incinerate the damned.

One man stared straight at me, and his eyes flashed as red as the coals. His eyes weren't just red; they were flaming coals that he aimed at me. They penetrated my spirit like the flaming arrows a barbarian shoots at his prey. I raced quickly inside and closed the door with a trembling hand but not forcefully enough to shut it properly.

I quickly entered the bedroom and pulled the large Quran off the shelf. Embracing it, I sat cross-legged in a corner as I attempted to invoke God's help in forgetting the appearance of that terrifying man and his demonic glare. But I didn't succeed in gaining control of myself or achieving even the least amount of calm and peace of mind. So, I started reciting to myself all the Quran's short chapters I had memorized, at a speed equaled only to the beats of my heart.

I hadn't finished reciting the chapter called "al-Nas" ("People"), when I heard my mother scream. I raced to her, clutching the Quran to my breast. I found her and my grandmother beating their chests and shrieking "Yabooo!" as my father, with another man, walked through the door, carrying my little brother whose scorched flesh had melted into his white *dishdasha*.[10]

I was in shock and raised a hand to my mouth, attempting to suppress the scream that was trying to emerge. The copy of the Quran fell from my hands, and I don't remember what happened to me after that.

All I remember of that day, before I fled to the roof terrace to hide, was that the door was wide open. I saw my father rush through it wearing mismatched plastic sandals of different sizes and colors. He carried back my charred baby brother as one of the men stood by the door of our house, mumbling words I couldn't hear. Two women – my mother and grandmother – were slapping their faces and chests and screaming bloody murder as the Quran landed on the floor.

I raced at top speed to the roof. I don't know whether I climbed the steps one at a time or in leaping strides. Even now, I can't remember how I made it to the roof. All I recall is the fiery heat that noon and how the terrace burned the soles of my feet. I looked around, searching everywhere but found no place to shelter from the terror of the scene, from my family, from the predatory eyes of the man who had glared at me, and from the heat of the roof, where I found no shade whatsoever.

I leaned against the wall, which transmitted its flaming heat to me the moment I touched it. I collapsed to the ground and sat cross-legged, trying as best I could to collect my spirit, which had evaporated from fear, but my heart kept beating faster and faster. I felt that something was almost suffocating me from inside. I didn't know its source, but it reached my heart and began pressing it hard. Then, I shrieked loudly with a voice I didn't recognize or understand how it became earsplitting enough to overwhelm the entire area and to reach the ears of my

---

[10] Dishdasha: A usually white, long robe for men, traditionally worn in the Middle East

grandmother, who appeared at the door to the roof, without her black scarf. She had also ripped the pocket from her blouse.

That moment lasted longer than all the prior years of my brief life. No matter how much I tried to make a sound or utter at least a single consonant, my voice had vanished, and my lips seemed cemented. Then, I felt faint.

My grandmother approached, took my hand, and raised me to my feet. Clasping her hand tight, I walked along with her, afraid of falling into an abyss that might gape open before me without warning. I moved slowly and shut my eyes, hoping that what had happened had been just a terrible nightmare that would disappear the moment I opened them.

I slept for an unknown length of time. When I eventually woke, I found the man with red eyes facing me. His eyes were even redder than before when he lurked beside a huge cauldron in which blood was boiling. As he extended his hand toward me, I noticed that his long fingernails were a disgusting black. His hand crept closer till it almost grabbed the hem of my *thobe*[11] where I sat cross-legged on the roof. I tried to escape his reach, but his hand slid ever nearer as I pressed my back repeatedly against the wall in the hope that I would break through it to prevent that terrifying hand from touching me. Not being able to evade it, I began to shriek: "Granny! Daddy, Mom, help me! He's going to burn me alive. Save me! He's going to set me on fire!"

"Calm down. Calm down. All power and might belong to Almighty God. What's become of us, my Lord?"

My grandmother comforted me and tried to wipe the sweat from my eyebrows. I struggled to compose myself and began to open my eyes, succeeding only with difficulty. Then, I found that my grandmother was patting my head with a cloth she had soaked in cold water.

---

[11] Thobe: A gownlike formal garment for men, worn primarily in the Arabian Peninsula. It is ankle-length and long-sleeved.

My father must also have come when he heard me scream. Standing near me, he asked, "How is she today?"

"Not as well as I would like. We'll need to take her to the doctor too," my grandmother replied.

"Her mother hasn't improved either, despite all the medicine she's taken," my father remarked in a voice as sad as my grandmother's.

"Listen, Son, may God help you in your trials: this is destiny. You and your wife are still in your prime. I feel certain that God will recompense you for the loss of your baby boy. Be patient, and don't forget that he has now become one of the birds of paradise. Don't exhaust yourself weeping for him; that won't help him in any way. Accept this catastrophe with a Believer's heart, and God will make it all up to you, Son. May God have mercy on all of us! All power and might belong to Almighty God. We'll wait till tomorrow morning. If your wife isn't better by then, put her in the hospital and stay there with her. I'll take care of Intisar till she recovers. Don't be angry at her. It's not her fault that she left the door open and that your son crawled outside. What happened, happened. Everything is predestined, my son. Don't let your anger at your daughter make a horrible situation worse."

I didn't hear any reply from my father but remember listening to his heavy, troubled footsteps when he left my side. I tried to fall asleep again, and found myself standing in the courtyard with my brother.

The courtyard of our house had no roof, and the sun's rays began to burn my head. I was almost vaporized by the heat, but my brother stood in the deep shadows of something I couldn't see. So, I began searching for him.

I was alarmed, however, when I saw that the house door was wide open. A tall man entered quickly and headed toward my brother, whom he picked up and carried away. I locked the two panels of the door and returned alone, as I shouted after the man: "Thief! Thief! My brother! Bring me back my brother! Don't burn him!"

A cooling cloud arrived and poured rain on my forehead. It actually wet my entire face. I woke up terrified only to discover my face was wet with cold water my grandmother had used to wash my face.

I tried to scrutinize her, but all I could see was a blurry image of her sorrowful face. I opened my mouth slowly, allowing drops of water to enter it. Then, I felt thirsty and wished to tell her I hadn't killed my brother. I mumbled some words that I think she didn't hear. She quickly picked up a glass of water with her left hand and brought it close to my mouth. I began to sip with my eyes half-closed.

I don't know whether I slept for three days or a week. I later heard that my mother spent an entire week in the hospital and that my father had stayed there with her. Meanwhile, my grandmother never left my side except to pray or relieve herself in the bathroom.

I wasn't convinced by the story I heard about my brother's death. Their summary version was that Salam had slipped out while my mother, who assumed the door to the house was shut tight, was busy cooking. She had gone to the kitchen to prepare our meal, as she did every day, and Salam crawled quickly to the door, which I had left open. At the doorstep, his *dishdasha* tripped him, and he toppled over the two benches there into the embers beneath one of the fiery cauldrons. Then, he was engulfed in flames before anyone noticed.

I was sure that the true cause of Salam's death was my being terrified by the man who glared at me with terrifying eyes. I had fled from him, without taking the time to close the door properly. When my brother found the door open, he poked his head outside. One of the men saw him, grabbed him, and threw him into the fire. So, he burned to death. Yes, I'm sure that's what actually happened, because . . . as my grandmother said, our neighbors are crooks who kill people for no reason at all.

My mother returned home once her health improved a bit, but her heart condition prevented her from taking charge of the household chores as she had previously done. She didn't smile

– not even when my father came home from work and complimented her sweetly.

The way my father treated me changed too. He no longer flattered me as he had before, and I felt shunned.

My mother collected all my brother's clothes and placed them in a cloth sack that she used as her pillow, even for her naps. I frequently saw her sniff that pillow while she wept.

My father did not hold a wake for my brother. Instead, each time he prayed he recited the sura named "Yasin" from the Quran on behalf of Salam's spirit. His sorrow left him looking like an old man, even after he shaved his beard, which had grown quickly when he returned to work after ten days, most of which he spent in the hospital with my mother. But his demeanor never resumed its previous appearance.

One day my father said, out of the blue, "I've rented a new house; we're moving there at the end of this month."

My mother protested angrily, "No, we'll never leave this house. Salam died here, and I will die here too."

Chapter

3

A Butterfly's Voice

Our new house was near Khan al-Makhdar in an area called "al-Madina Street". It was an Iraqi courtyard house that contained several rooms, a bathroom, and a toilet – arranged around a small circular patio that lacked a roof.

So, our new house had three rooms that adjoined each other, a bathroom under the stairs, a toilet by the main entrance, and three separate roof terraces. The first terrace was small and held a *tannur*, an earthen oven for baking bread. The middle terrace had a locked room where the owners' effects were stored, while they lived in Baghdad. The top terrace was like a paradise no outsider could reach. I began to escape there around five in the afternoon and would stay there till my mother went to bed on the second roof, which was a quiet place for all of us to sleep and escape from the summer's fiery heat.

In the courtyard, the roofless part of the house, our family experienced the climate's peculiarities firsthand. Cold, or alternatively heat, crept unobstructed into every nook there, and dust storms permeated every inch of the area with vicious force. The doors of the house could not withstand them either.

After each sandstorm, the entire house had to be cleaned thoroughly, even if the storm had not caused any damage. Persistent rain was a genuine disaster we couldn't avoid in the winter.

After initially ruling out the idea of moving, my mother finally yielded to my father's decision and my grandmother's pleas. She agreed to move, but only grudgingly.

We transported our possessions in a large, open truck, which followed the taxi that transported us to our new house. The building stood by a sidewalk parallel to the main street, where some of my father's relatives had lived for a long time. I soon started to refer to them as "Uncle" and "Aunt." Their sons were just my age, but their daughters were too young to be my playmates.

My grandmother soon met a woman her age, and they began to meet at our house every day; each told the other woman her life stories.

When she felt well enough, my mother occupied herself by reading the Quran. When she was indisposed, she rested in bed while we gathered around her and discussed cheerful subjects, trying to lift her spirits. We occasionally succeeded, but all too often our efforts met with devastating failure. After examining our faces one by one, she would turn to face the wall and begin weeping quietly.

Once the summer ended and clouds covered the entire sky, we finally brought our pallet beds down from the roof. Then, my father locked the metal doors to the three roofs.

"Winter's just around the corner," my grandmother remarked as she gazed up at the sky, which was blanketed by black clouds.

Smiling, my father replied, "No, it has arrived." Then, he picked up his cotton mattress and carried it to his room.

Trying to inhale deeply, my mother observed, "At least we've escaped from the heat."

I remember being amazed to see all those black clouds rest motionlessly over the roof of our house, as if they were all glued to each other.

"At this time of the year, in the eighth month, there's no guarantee it will actually rain," my mother commented to my grandmother.

Rising with difficulty, my grandmother replied, "The matter's in God's hands."

We had no sooner gone inside than all at once rain began to fall in torrents – as if it had been waiting for us to take cover before pouring down ferociously. I stood at the window looking at the courtyard which was paved with medium-sized, orange-colored tiles. So much rain fell that the drains could not handle all the water.

Then, water rose high enough in the courtyard to follow us inside, slipping through the gap beneath the closed doors and wetting the carpets and pallets, which we then placed on top of the wooden wardrobes in which we stored our clothes.

We became anxious and nervous about what would become of us if the rain continued relentlessly. Then, my grandmother suggested we spend the remainder of the day with our relatives. I had thought of breaking the lock to the room on the roof and staying there. I dismissed that idea, though, when I remembered the large crack that ran all the way from top to bottom of one of the walls which I feared might collapse.

After the downpour had continued for a long time, everyone agreed to leave and visit our nearby relatives, whose living space had a different floor plan. My grandmother quickly pulled out three foam mats, rolled them up, and asked us to shove one under the door of each of our rooms to keep rain from flooding our house in our absence.

I helped my father, mother, and grandmother fold these mats and push them under the doors. Then, we locked the entry door securely and ran quickly through the heavy rain to our relative Umm Faris' house, where this short, plump, fair-skinned, cheerful woman who greeted us with a smile, urging us to go inside quickly. When she noticed how wet we were, she brought us clean towels to dry off.

"I'll bring you some clothes," Umm Faris offered.

"Oh, don't worry about us. We brought an overnight bag," my father replied.

She fed us bread and fried eggs for supper, and we drank tea, after we changed into dry clothes from the medium-sized, leather suitcase my father had referred to as an "overnight bag". It also contained my mother's medicines and a clean sheet.

My aunt, Umm Faris, took our wet clothes and hung them to dry on a clothesline in a covered courtyard.

That night, I heard a lot as I listened to these relatives talk. Their stories differed a lot from the conversations of my family, who feared the future. Like us, my uncle's family was poor, but in their faces, I didn't detect the anxiety I encountered daily in my father's overall appearance, or the sorrow in my mother's eyes, or the despair that clouded my grandmother's.

Everyone in this family seemed happy. My Uncle Abu Faris, as I started to call him, was a thin policeman and older than my father. His twin sons, Faris and Hazim, got along famously. Their sister, who was over four, was handicapped and could not walk unassisted.

When I asked one of the boys about his school, he complained: "School is boring, and our subjects are really hard."

The other boy added quickly, "The principal is cranky and hateful."

I didn't ask them about the girls' school and decided to check it out myself, especially since the summer vacation had almost ended.

After supper I helped my Aunt Umm Faris with the dishes. She was really happy about that – as she told me – because, since she had married, no one had ever helped her clean the house or wash the dishes. I was delighted to hear her tell my mother, "Umm Intisar, congratulations on your daughter, Intisar!"

My mother smiled, and I thought she looked proud when she glanced at me as I returned from the kitchen. This time, I slept near my grandmother as usual but in the same room with my father and mother.

"Intisar, Intisar! Come on! Get up! Quick! Try not to disturb the others," my father whispered as he tried to wake me up.

"What is it, Daddy? Why are you waking me up now, when I'm so sleepy?" I asked, yawning.

"Come quick! Put on your shoes quickly, before anyone else hears us."

"Shoes? My shoes are in our house. I left them there yesterday."

"Never mind then. Put your sandals on and come. Come quick, before any of the others wakes up."

I had no idea what time it was when we left that house, but the sun had risen, and the sky was clear; only tufts of cotton clouds were scattered here and there.

My father didn't use the key to open the door to our house – a strong shove sufficed. When I looked inside, my mouth gaped open, and I felt queasy. A strong stench rose till it reached my mouth and streamed out as vomit.

My father grasped my head with a hand to lean it forward. He held my back with his other hand and said, "Calm down. Stay calm." I continued throwing up, though.

So, he quickly pulled me away from the open door and sat me down on the sidewalk. He asked me to breathe deeply. I did, as he watched me anxiously. I soon stopped vomiting and tried to distract myself by gazing up at the sky and then at my father.

He gave me a choice: "If you feel better now but can't help me do this, go back. But don't tell anyone what you've seen – not even your grandmother!"

"No, I'm fine. I'll help you, Daddy," I replied as I tried to stand and shake off the sidewalk's dirt from my dress.

"In that case, take this aluminum bowl and do as I do."

Clutching another aluminum bowl, my father entered the house, and I followed him cautiously, holding the bowl he had given me.

The floors of the living areas and the kitchen – its door open – were completely covered with coffee-colored turds that floated on the surface of the water. They must have spilled from the backed-up toilet when the sewer line overflowed because of the heavy rain the day before.

At first, I was almost suffocated by the stink. Trying to pull myself together, I stopped breathing through my nostrils. I clenched my teeth together in disgust, though, when I saw my father scoop up a pile of turds with his bowl and carry them to a large sheet of aluminum near the doorstep.

He continued to plow the river of turds, going up one row at a time, collecting as much shit as his little bowl could hold before he emptied it all out.

I closed my eyes and pursed my lips before I attacked the mound of turds near my feet. I scooped them up and hurried away before the stench entered my nostrils. I had to open my eyes though, for fear of falling.

I walked outside cautiously and added my catch to the pile, which was almost entirely covered with shit and polluted water.

"Put it all there," my father said, pointing to another sheet a short distance from the first.

So, I emptied my bowl. I hadn't understood before what it was doing on the roof terrace of the house near the earthenware oven.

I collected lots of turds. Each time I returned to the house, I walked cautiously to keep from falling. By the time we filled six tin cans that had previously held a vegetable oil called al-Ra'I – as the labels indicated, the place was almost cleaned out. There were only three heaps next to each other in the middle of the house. Then, my father went to clean the shit off the kitchen floor; we hadn't blocked its door with a sponge mat as we had done for the bedrooms.

This time, I took off my sandals and walked quickly to the turd heaps to scoop them up with my bowl, but the floor was covered with water so stinky it clogged up my nostrils. So, I lost my balance and fell, sliding across the floor.

My father raced out of the kitchen and lifted me by my armpits. Opening the bathroom door, he carried me into it and sat me on its wooden bench. He told me: "Clean up. I'll bring you another *thobe*."

He closed the bathroom door after turning on the light. I couldn't look up at my father when I noticed the bottom of my *thobe* was soiled because of the dirty water and the smear from the turds, which clung to it. The stench emanating from me clung to me, to my very pores once the bathroom door was shut.

I felt ashamed of myself and despised this house, which was awash with shit. I cursed poverty, which had denied us a house with a roof over the courtyard. Most of all, I felt an intense hatred for the rain.

Hot tears poured from my eyes down to my cheeks, where they mixed with the shower's cold water that fell mercilessly on my head and left me shivering from the cold. Once I smelled the soap I used to scrub my body with, trying to remove all traces of the stench, the nauseating stains and taste of poverty, I forgot how cold the water was.

I put on the clean *thobe* my father brought me, after I dried my hair and body thoroughly with a dry towel that was hanging in the bathroom.

"Don't tell anyone what we've done!" my father said, not just once but twice. "I'm now going to carry the aluminum sheets to that wrecked house over there. Wait here for me."

I felt ashamed of my weak body when I saw my father lift those panels one after another with difficulty, carrying them a good distance away from our house. He covered them with the wet foam mats, which he weighed down with some broken bricks and planks he found around the demolished building.

He checked and double-checked to make sure the wind wouldn't be able to blow the covers off and reveal our secret. If it did, we would find ourselves in a cumbersome situation.

He hurriedly entered our house where he picked out clean, dry clothes and entered the bathroom. I left the entry door open and sat on the steps in front of it, keeping an eye on our secret sheets, for fear some intruder would approach and uncover them.

"You go back to Aunt Umm Faris' house, and I'll find a guy with a barrel to haul the sheets out of the city before too many flies flock on them." He gestured toward their temporary hiding place.

He was trying to dry his hair while he spoke. Then, he put a hand in his pocket to search for his wallet. When he didn't find it, he rushed to his room, after returning the towel to the bathroom. He reappeared immediately, closed the entry door, locked it, and left.

I didn't feel I could barge into our relatives' house, because I didn't want to wake them by knocking on the door. Leaving early that morning, I had shut it quietly behind me.

I also could not go back inside our house, because my father had locked its door. So, I sat on the curb and watched the flies that had started to gather on those shitty sheets, now that their stench was broadcasting our secret.

A Butterfly's Voice

Chapter

4

A Butterfly's Voice

One Wednesday morning, someone knocked on our door, and I opened the door to find a huge, bare-headed woman with a scary face standing before me. She wore a light blue blouse and a long black skirt. She was carrying a black leather bag by a strap over her shoulder. Beside her stood a plump, bald man wearing white shirt and black trousers. A large suitcase rested against him. When the woman smiled at me, I saw a gold tooth in her upper jaw.

In a husky voice the woman inquired: "This is Abu Intisar's house, isn't it?"

"Yes," I replied nervously as I stared at her frightening face, which looked more like a man's, except that her long hair fell to her shoulders.

"Sweetie, is he home now?" the man asked me affectionately.

I quickly closed the door on them and raced inside, calling to my father. He hastily opened the door again, welcomed them, and invited the couple inside, while I sped to my mother and grandmother, who were donning their abayas.

Once he was seated, the man explained, "We haven't come to collect the rent. Instead, we want to fix the drains and the sewer line for this house. As you know, Abu Intisar, this house belongs to some orphans, and we are holding it in trust for them till they come of age. Since you are a Believer, you understand the significance of a trust."

"Certainly," my father replied.

"Some of our belongings are stored in the upstairs room. I believe you have the key, don't you?" the man asked my father.

"Yes, I do. Shall I bring it?"

The woman said, "My brother, Abu Ala', and I will spend a day or two with you. We'll sleep in that room and supervise the workmen. Once the work is completed, we'll return, God willing, to Baghdad."

We were all confused, and our astonishment showed clearly on our faces. We didn't understand how a man could share a room with his sister.

"As you wish," my father responded with hesitation.

My grandmother, though, whispered to my mother, "Strange!"

My father fetched the key to the room and gave it to the landlady from Baghdad. Our guests drank the tea that my mother made for them, and I quickly served. Then, the woman asked me to bring her a broom and a rag so she could clean the room.

I began to draw a picture to distract myself from the face of that woman who was cleaning the room upstairs together with her brother. Without meaning to, I drew a face with facial features resembling hers.

My mother prepared lunch for the two guests, who came downstairs to eat. That afternoon, the man and my father went out to locate a contractor and workers who could install the new pipes to reconnect our house to the sewer. The woman returned to their room and stayed there until the two men returned with a contractor, who inspected the sewer lines. Then, the woman negotiated the cost of the work with that contractor.

Despite their visit, my grandmother didn't forsake her daily custom of spreading her cotton mattress and mine over the walls of the terrace on sunny days to – as she put it – disinfect them. She would take them up there as soon as we woke up, and I would bring them down from the roof before sunset.

Our two guests spent the next couple of days checking on the workmen as the project progressed, and my mother and grandmother cooked for them. In the evening, they would go to the room upstairs and spend the night there.

My mother noticed that the woman hadn't changed her clothes since she arrived. Why then, if she did not plan to change her clothes, had she brought a large suitcase? But she didn't bring up this topic with my father, and instead, discussed it with my grandmother.

By the evening of the third day, the workmen connected the pipes of our house to the sewer line, removed the debris from the street, received their pay, and left. My father and Abu Ala' went into the bathroom to check if everything functioned properly, and the woman went up to their room as usual. My grandmother was busy preparing to pray as was my mother.

Meanwhile, I was watching the cartoons that were broadcast at six, immediately after daily recitations from the Holy Quran. When my grandmother finished her prayers and the children's programs ended, she asked me to bring our pallets back down from the roof. Then, as she did each evening, she began to recite passages from the Quran.

I climbed the steps quietly to avoid disturbing our guests. When I came close to the wall where our mattresses aired, I tried to pull one of them down to place it over my shoulder – as I did every evening, I heard the woman moan. I could make out other noises I had never heard before.

I felt alarmed at first and guessed that Abu Ala' was kneeling over the woman and trying to strangle her, while she struggled to push his hands off her neck.

I dismissed that notion when the sounds momentarily ceased. But I soon heard those noises again. I stretched to put the pallet back on the wall and tiptoed to the room's locked door.

When I peeked through the keyhole, I began to tremble, and my heart pounded faster. Although my throat was parched, sweat dripped from my forehead. After a fleeting look, I raced back to the pallets, quickly pulled both of them off the wall, put them over my shoulders, and raced down the steps.

I tried to erase that terrible sight from my eyes but couldn't. When my grandmother came to call me to supper, I pretended to be asleep.

The couple left the next morning, thanking my mother and grandmother for their impeccable hospitality. They handed the room key to my father before they left. When I glanced at the suitcase, I noticed – from the way they carried it – that it seemed empty.

At noon, we gathered around the lunch tray and started discussing our recent guests. While chewing on my food, my grandmother observed, "A sister didn't used to share a room with her brother. Apparently, customs have changed nowadays."

My mother added, "Umm Sa'd never changed her clothes the entire time she was here. Why did she bring a large suitcase then? Do you suppose it was full of something else?"

My father was startled and seemed to have grasped something that had eluded him till that moment. He shot a look at my mother, rushed to his room to fetch the key to the room upstairs and raced up the stairs. When he returned moments later, his face was distorted with anger. He then declared: "I'm no pimp!"

My grandmother asked right away, "Abu Intisar, what are you saying?" Meanwhile, my mother covered her mouth in a frenzy. It was obvious that she couldn't believe my father had actually said that.

He was so furious that he turned around and around as he tried to find his sandals. He left the house muttering words I didn't understand, and I ran to close the door he had left ajar. Then, as we ate in silence, I watched my mother and grandmother communicate with only their eyes.

We finished the meal without uttering a word. When we were done, my mother took my father's plate and put it in the fridge while I went to the kitchen, planning to wash the dishes. Before I could start, there was a knock on the door, and I realized my father had returned. I ran to let him in and found there was another man with him. Before they came inside, my father asked us to go to our bedroom. My mother and grandmother obeyed and headed to my grandmother's room.

I stood my ground, and the two men climbed to the roof, where they stayed for some time. By eavesdropping from the bottom of the stairs, I was able to make out some broken sentences from their heated conversation.

I quickly ran to the kitchen when I heard them descend. Through the window, I saw them carrying three plastic bags of different colors. My father had a bag in each hand, and the other man carried the third.

In a loud, angry voice my father declared, "This is the proof, Abu Dargham. Empty bottles. I'm moving out of this house at the end of the month. I won't stay here any longer. I've paid the rent for this month to fix the drains but won't stay beyond that. What does that slut think?"

The man tried to appease my father and promised to find him another house by the month's end. After seeing him off, my father tossed the bottles in the trash can so hard that I heard some of them break.

My father was furious all day long because he had found the empty wine bottles that Umm Sa'd and Abu Ala' had left in their room. I was the only one in our family, though, who knew the whole story.

When I was on the roof trying to take our mattresses off the wall, I had heard loud groans and a man and woman huffing and puffing. Curiosity had inspired me to trace the origin of those noises to the door of the room upstairs and to look through the keyhole. My eyes were glued on two totally naked bodies on top of a large pallet. I watched the woman's massive white body as she raised her legs, which were spread wide open, while from her sweaty face, her hair cascaded. She was clasping the waist of the plump man, who was persistently attempting to squeeze his entire naked body between her huge legs.

I had fled quickly from the roof for fear they would notice me and sense the eyes spying on them from outside. I had quickly pulled the mattresses off the wall and gone hiding downstairs.

I didn't sleep that night; I usually did not whenever I encountered something different or spotted something I hadn't witnessed before. I had never seen even a still photo of two people having sex, not in a magazine or a book; so, how could I fathom a scene like this, especially since I had never imagined my mother and father making love. Not even my grandmother had told me what the word "sex" meant – if only because I had never asked her. All I knew was that my father and mother shared a bedroom and a bed. But I had never wondered whether they did in bed what our guests had done.

Did my mother strip naked and spread her legs to receive my father? Did she have to? If so, why? What did she experience when she did? What did my father feel when he was on top of her?

The many questions that swirled in my head kept suggesting new queries, none of which I could answer. A strange sensation overwhelmed me – one I didn't understand. I felt a mixture of loathing, hatred, and disrespect toward my father and mother, so profound that I couldn't bring myself to look at either of them throughout the next day.

All these images kept merging in my head whenever I tried to sleep. I visualized my mother naked on a coarse rug while my father, who was also naked, lay on top of her, and laughed and laughed as he feverishly tried to penetrate her body. She was pleading with me with her eyes, asking me to save her from this foreign object lodged in her body. But then, metal bars rose quickly to separate me from her.

When I clutched a bar with both hands and began screaming, my terrified grandmother woke up and scrambled toward me, reciting the "Yasin"-sura from the Quran while she stroked my head. She assumed I had been affected by the contaminating presence in our home of the two guests and the wine. So, she tried to ward off this evil by reciting the *Fatiha*[12] one hundred and twenty times over water that she sprinkled on the walls and throughout all the corners of our house. But my nightmares continued for months.

---

[12] Fatiha: Quran's first short sura, which is an essential element of ritual prayer for Muslims.

Chapter

5

A Butterfly's Voice

My father had trouble finding a new house for us, much more trouble than he had when he was looking for our two previous houses. Faced by a self-imposed deadline at the end of the month, he searched extensively and was clearly exhausted whenever he came back from yet another expedition. He didn't merely spend time with people who might know of a house fit for a family, he walked the city's streets, far and wide, searching for an empty house.

Every day, he returned to utter the same words: "I didn't find a house," until the twenty-fifth of the month when he smiled to signal that we have a new house. To us, however, his news merely meant having to begin the work of bundling up our possessions once again and packing small, necessary items like glassware and kitchen utensils in cardboard boxes of various sizes.

My grandmother was upset to leave the neighbor she had befriended here, but when my father noticed her sad expression, he told her: "Don't fret. Our new house isn't very far from here. It's at the end of the second street. The owners live nearby. I'm forced to rent it, even though I don't want to become . . ."

My father didn't finish that sentence when he noticed I was watching him attentively.

"Praise God!" my grandmother said. She was happy to know that she wouldn't be separated from her new friend. My father added that the house layout had some challenges. While it had two rooms with a concrete roof, another roofed section couldn't be used, because one of the walls there was structurally unsound. Anyone who saw the roof of our house from the street would think it was fine, but inside, one post was badly compromised.

After my father described the condition of the house he had rented, my mother observed sadly, "Poor folks always have sub-standard homes." My father instructed me adamantly not to go on the roof lest I fall.

I obeyed his order, and my grandmother also gave up her habit of spreading the pallets and covers on the walls of the roof. Whenever I wanted to be alone, I would climb to the top step of the stairs and listen to the stillness of the space surrounding me there.

I never cared to meet the neighborhood girls my age or the many boys who played marbles in the street every afternoon, when they competed to see who could collect the most marbles and be crowned the victor. The actual winner, though, was the owner of the small shop that sold those small, colorful, translucent balls they played with, turning them with a strong tap from their index and middle fingers. Young girls played hopscotch, which they called *tuki* or *muhallaqu*. They drew ten squares, numbered them, and advanced a piece of a broken tile from one square to the next while hopping on one foot. The winner was the girl who made it all the way through the course without a misstep. Then, she would choose one of the squares as her base and ask the other girls to hop over it on one foot. They usually started playing in the afternoon and continued till the sunset prayer, when everyone went home.

Oddly enough, I didn't see any of the girls who lived on our street at my new school. This middle school wasn't very far from our house, but I liked to wake up early to watch the world come to life. I really wanted to rise before life itself did, and thus, to discover which dove was the first to stir the day and whether the eucalyptus tree on the far side of the pavement stretched its branches when it woke up.

When I entered my new school, I noticed its fragrance differed from that of my primary school; it was more acrid. All the pupils I saw here wore the same uniform, which consisted of a dark blue smock that reached below the knee, a white blouse, short white socks, and black shoes with low heels. So, all the girls could have easily been the same pupil duplicated many times over, but with different faces.

I always wore white ribbons on my braided hair, which reached down to my waist. So, the other girls referred to me as "the kid." Most of them used hairpins of different colors and sizes to hold their hair up.

Unlike the pupils in my former school, the girls here weren't amiable, quiet, or obedient. They were rebels who were always ready to cause problems and start a quarrel. They frequently sought ways to stand out and assert their dominance. Each girl strove to establish she was superior to the others.

I was delighted by my nickname – "the kid," because it was an improvement over my previous ones, "the adult" or "the only child" (after my brother died).

I began to play the role of a little girl the moment I reached the school. Once I entered the school's portal, I suddenly turned into a little girl.

Even my teachers noticed that I didn't act like the other pupils, that I seemed more innocent than the others. My homeroom teacher told me I focused mindfully on the details of the lessons.

I always sought answers to my questions, which centered on the day's instruction.

I began to feel that everyone was pampering me when gradually the other students' dislike of me, which I had felt the first three days, turned into a tepid love. Their affection for me was conditional on my not revealing their little secrets about things that happened in class. I duly obeyed that rule, because such matters were, first and last, no concern of mine.

The first twenty days, I woke up early – at times, very early – and ate breakfast, consisting of a triangular piece of cheese and *samuna*[13], or a hardboiled egg and a glass of tea. Then, I would hoist my heavy schoolbag over my right shoulder and head out. The moment I pulled my abaya over my head, I would discover I had become a poised, adult woman who shouldn't transgress or violate any rule decreed for her, no matter what. So, I would begin to agonize over those stifling rules.

Whenever I tried to drive them from my mind with a brisk shake of my head, their voice grew louder and echoed lethally. Speaking loudly on the street was forbidden. Chewing

---

[13] Samuna: a loaf of round bread, largely consumed in the Middle East

gum in public was forbidden. Laughing or smiling was forbidden. Looking at the faces of passersby was forbidden.

The word "forbidden" (*mamnu'*) haunted me from the moment I left the doorstep of our house all the way to the school's fence. Once I was on school grounds, it took on a different aspect – one I could at least tolerate – because "forbidden" there meant cheating on exams, wearing high heels, and taking a snack or a drink into a classroom.

Because I was "the little kid" here, if only because that was what everyone called me, I assumed that identity the moment I removed my abaya. I became a capricious girl with white ribbons. Occasionally, I would forget who I was and start sucking on my right thumb, like a nursing infant.

Chapter

6

A Butterfly's Voice

On the first morning of the eighth month of 1980, I went to school as usual. As part of our daily routine, we all stood to perform the morning salute, but the atmosphere was different. The teachers had anxious, worried, apprehensive expressions on their faces, like those I had recently begun to observe on my parents.

When the principal appeared and stood at the center of the rows of students, she did not discuss the usual – repeated absences of some students, violations of the dress code, or cleanliness. She actually skipped her weekly customary speech about breaking some girls' high heels and forcing them to walk barefoot the rest of the school day.

That was the first time I had seen her arrive without the heavy stick she used to cane lazy pupils with. Her eyes lacked their normal ferocity. All the girls stared at her lips as they tried to guess what our chauvinistic Kurdish principal would say. In her gray skirt and black jacket, she looked sterner than ever. Her posture differed too from her customary Thursday morning stance. Her body language suggested she was anxious, apprehensive, and fearful. Her voice lacked control and was lifeless. She did her best to stand erect, and within five minutes, adopted a military stance. When she started to speak, she sounded listless. Her words fell on my ears like an echo.

"My dear pupils, our school will close for ten days, beginning today, until the evil 'Zoroastrian' war that Iran has launched against our mighty Iraq ends. Victory will be ours, thanks to our militant commander, Saddam Hussein. May God preserve and protect him! You will now return to your classes, and each class supervisor will guide you to an orderly exit through the school's door. I will meet you again, God willing, in ten days, after our victory."

Many pupils relished the idea of returning home and staying there, liberated from instruction and homework. A few girls began to think out loud about the new words they had heard that day. None of us had expected that such terrifying words would haunt us for the rest of our lives.

All the way home I asked myself what "victory" meant and how it would be achieved?

Returning home that day was frighteningly different; the streets were almost deserted, and the air was stifling, even though it was still morning. I sensed that something was about to happen. I wondered whether it would affect everyone or just me. Would it affect my family?

When I reached home, before my family had time to be surprised by my early return, I repeated to them what the principal had told us. After my report, I asked a number of questions. "What does 'victory' mean? How will Iraq be victorious? Why must there be a war between us and Iran? Will this war actually be over in ten days?"

My grandmother ran to me and placed her hand over my mouth. She whispered to me that no one knew the answer to any of these questions.

I no longer felt like watching cartoons on TV. In fact, I no longer felt like watching television at all, because it became a window onto death, which had donned khaki clothes. The calm television music had been replaced by harsh voices, endless angry speeches, and patriotic songs.

Clad in an army uniform, the president appeared on the screen at least once a day. We frequently saw him several times during a single day. The period of ten days passed, but the war did not. Then, we returned to school, but it had also become another screen for television's scary, hateful faces.

Now, every day, we had to attend the principal's address, which was copied from the president's speeches. Afterwards, one of the school's male employees, wearing a military uniform, would head to the *dais*[14] near the flag and fire several rounds from his rifle.

Each time he fired a shot, some pupils trembled in fear. Unlike those girls who succumbed to patriotic fervor whenever

---

[14] Dais: A low platform

they heard shots being fired and who then began to scream, "Long live the Commander! Long live the Commander!" I was almost suffocated by the smell of gunpowder and would try to hide from it behind some of the taller girls. This attempt always failed miserably; that smell seemed to be telling me: "I'll find you wherever you try to hide. You can never escape."

Little by little, the war infiltrated our days in school as each teacher was obliged to repeat the news about our fearless forces and the victory they would shortly achieve before classes began. In my head, however, raced the images of the TV news presenters I had seen the previous night before I fell asleep. Those replaced my teachers' faces in school the next morning.

A disgusting new assignment was added to our daily homework: we were required to memorize portions of the president's speeches and to discuss these in a class called "National Education," which was now required from every pupil every day. We complied and repeated like parrots, faster or slower, what we had memorized. I tried unsuccessfully to understand what was being said then.

I completed middle school with distinction, and my classmates were impressed by my seriousness about studying and especially how I had been able to obtain such high marks in these exceptional wartime conditions, which hadn't improved. The fact of the matter was that I succeeded in my studies because I was afraid of the war. Yes, I feared it so much that I was terrified by the thought of the unpredictable future awaiting me and my family. What might become of us when they conscripted my father and he died in the war? Would we become homeless? Who would pay the rent for our house? What if a rocket fell on our house or our school or our street? What if? What if? What if? Whenever these alarming ideas filled my head, I would flee from them by turning to my school books.

One day when I was exhausted from studying and had gone to bed early in my grandmother's room, while everyone else was watching TV, I heard a voice through the window, which was open to the street. Then, wondering who was speaking, I looked around to make sure I wasn't dreaming. The voice repeated his words: "Hafiz, this war won't ever end. Believe me."

Another voice replied sadly, "I know, Amin. I know that, believe me. But what will we do to survive?"

"Listen. My father said that they won't conscript a student with excellent marks but will conscript a student who fails the exams as soon as he turns eighteen. I want to excel so they won't drag me away to this damn war before I have a chance to live." He uttered the last phrase in a weeping voice.

"I don't like studying. I hate it. I'm going to flee Iraq. One of my cousins has lived in Bologna for a long time. I'm going to leave this place and live there with him."

"How are you going to escape? Escaping this place is impossible. Be realistic."

"Don't mock my dreams. Yes, I will escape because I don't want to die. Do you understand me?"

"I wish you the best of luck with your plan, but mine is to excel in my studies and find deliverance from the war this way. I'll study from nine at night to four in the morning. Then, I'll sleep till seven, when I review what I studied, before going to school."

"Do what you want, but as for me, I'm definitely leaving."

This conversation seeped into my soul like water into arid soil. I was in urgent need of a plan, and I followed the steps exactly as I had heard them. When I returned from school, I would eat, help my mother with the chores, and nap till nine p.m.

Then, I would wash my face to fully wake up and study. Many nights, I studied till after five a.m. and slept only till seven, when I headed off to school, dragging my body there while trying to wrap my mind around the academic material I had stuffed into it.

I paid no attention to the streets, which were almost deserted in the morning, and separated myself from the children's hubbub in the afternoon. I succeeded brilliantly. In fact, I had the top scores in the entire city at the middle school level. At the time, I had no goal I was working toward and had adopted no plan for my future, but I became extremely angry when my father informed me that my academic standing entitled me to be admitted to my city's Teacher Training Institute. Before he had even finished his sentence, I fled to the bedroom where I started to cry. I didn't know why I was weeping but I wept a lot.

Suddenly, unexpectedly, everyone became interested in my future, even my school's principal. I was baffled; what was this future they were discussing? I was amazed that they didn't realize that in a time of war, there can be no future.

I didn't discuss my future, which I had begun to feel was looking bleak. I left it to my father to decide what I should be while I focused on the remainder of the school vacation, which seemed long and boring. I forgot about books, exams, and good grades. I was assailed instead by a greater anxiety, which I didn't call existential for fear that people would laugh at me. Because I couldn't hide it, though, everyone began to ask me, "What's wrong with you? What's happening to you?" Should I have just said, "Nothing" and lied?

One evening, my father approached me while I sat staring at the TV, and said, "Try to wake up early tomorrow. I'm going to take you somewhere."

I got up early, and we left the house together, walking side by side: a father and his very young daughter. We entered a building I had never seen before and headed to a room with a closed door. He knocked softly on it. A friendly lady opened it and greeted him with a lovely smile. She told us, "Please come in."

After we both entered, he replied, "This is my daughter. She passed the exams with high marks and will become a teacher, God willing."

"Ma sha' Allah. She looks bright," the lady said in her pleasant voice.

My father took my hand tenderly and led me toward bookcases that emitted a new, unfamiliar fragrance. "You will read all these books," he said. "Choose any of them you want."

"Children's books are on this side, and young adult books are on the other," the woman said, trying to guide me to those shelves.

In a calm voice, I said, "I want this book", as I pointed to a volume that contained both *Al-Nazarat* and *Al-'Abarat* (*Views* and *Tears*) by al-Manfaluti.

The woman gave my father a surprised look, but he told her: "Please, check this book out to me. I'll sign for it." Then, he went off to perform the chore he had come for while I stayed in the library and read.

By the time my father returned to take me home, I had read fifteen pages of the book. Even though I hadn't understood everything, I was a different person from the girl who had arrived there that morning.

Something inside me had matured, something that allowed me to develop quickly into a grown woman in a girl's body. On our way home, my shadow was no longer shorter than my father's. It had grown as tall as his.

Something that tasted both sweet and sour stirred inside me and lent significance to everything I saw. I quickly finished the second book my father borrowed for me but soon discovered that reading didn't quench my thirst. In fact, it made me thirstier. Everything I read increased the aridity in my spirit and I seemed distracted.

I began blaming myself for not discovering this pleasure before, because I should have begun reading on my own before middle school. I was very sad to discover this large void in my spirit and grew obsessed with the idea of reading all the books other readers praised. I paid no attention to a book's size or the number of its pages; if someone praised it, saying it was "very good," that meant I wouldn't go to bed that night before I had tucked it snugly under my pillow after leafing carefully through its pages.

All the same, I noticed something important: the more I read, the larger the library collections grew and the thirstier my spirit became. How could I quench this thirst? Who could offer me advice? Who would take my head between their hands and offer me some relief from my obsession?

Day by day, I lost my appetite for food.

We returned to school, and I kept asking the Arabic language teacher more questions about the most important books to read. She, however, tailored her responses to my stage of life, gender, and religion, and so eventually suggested that I read young adult books.

The phrase "young adult books," which I had heard from both the librarian and my teacher, lodged in my mind, accompanied by a big question mark. I began to wonder whether it referred to a special type of book or writer.

One day, I entered the room I shared with my grandmother and found her listening to the voice of a Quran reciter on the radio. Only her body was present, because her spirit and mind were roaming in other, non-physical realms. She was smiling, and her eyes filled with tears as she listened with every pore of her body to that voice.

Amazing! How intimately my grandmother knows God!

The moment the voice said, "God Almighty has spoken rightly," I quickly told her, "Granny, I want to see God."

My question didn't surprise her. In fact, she gazed at me compassionately and replied, "You couldn't cope with such a sight."

"I'm strong."

"Each of us believes that, but it's not simply a matter of strength or weakness. It depends entirely on what is concealed here." She pointed to her chest.

"What's that?"

"Something called faith. Its strength is what determines your ability to see His light, may He be glorified and exalted."

"Granny, you don't understand. I want to see God, not His light."

"But He is the light. He says in the holy book:

'God is the light of the heavens and the earth. His light is like a niche with a lamp inside it. This lamp is in a glass container. The glass is like a brilliant star. The lamp's fuel is oil from a blessed tree, which is neither eastern nor western. Its oil is luminous even before it is lit. Light on light. God guides to His light whom He wishes. God provides metaphors for people. God is omniscient'."[15]

"Granny, you are scaring me!"

"Why are you scared? There is nothing in this Quranic verse that should arouse fear. It is exceptionally beautiful. Listen, young lady, I know you possess something we no longer have. We lost it long ago; I mean innocence. You possess this gem. Use your innocence. Plead with Him. Ask Him for that. Say: 'Lord, I want to see You.' Then wait; you will find that His response is perfect."

I told myself before I fell asleep that I was ready to see Him. I stretched out in bed, gazed at the ceiling, and whispered, "My glorious Lord, allow me to see You!"

I didn't sleep at all that night, as I waited for something to happen . . . for hours. It was almost morning when my body began to feel numb. Then, I yielded to slumber's delight and dozed off.

Two very powerful hands grabbed my shoulders and shook them so fiercely that I was scared. I heard a voice rising from an unknown depth say: "Open your eyes. He is here. Look at Him."

I wasn't able to open my eyes. Light coated my eyelids and wove my eyelashes together so tightly I couldn't separate them to look at the source of that light or search for the source of that voice. My whole being dissolved, and I wasn't conscious of where I was till I heard my mother, who was trying to wake me up.

"Wake up, Darling. What's wrong? Do you have a fever?"

I pressed my head to her chest and burst into tears.

---

[15] Quran 24: 35

My grandmother normally bathed each Friday before the noon prayer. Occasionally, she would rise early to rinse her braids with henna and then wait a few hours before bathing. She would remind everyone before she entered the bathroom, "Bathing on Friday is obligatory, not discretionary."

She observed this custom except during cold winter days, but today she didn't get up early for her ritual. In fact, when I woke up, she quickly opened the chest containing her clothes and pulled out a white cloak that had holy verses written on it with yellow ink. She started to try it on. Then, she looked at me and said, "If your mother's awake, ask her to come to me now."

"Of course, Granny."

I went and called my mother, who came quickly. "What's happening?" she asked.

"Listen: he's coming to take me today."

I interrupted my grandmother: "Who? Who's coming?"

"Your grandfather," she replied.

My mother closed her eyes from which tears were flowing profusely.

"Daddy, Daddy!" I screamed as I ran to his room.

My father woke up in alarm. "What's wrong with you? Why are you screaming? What's happened?"

"I don't know. Granny's leaving, and Mama's weeping."

"Leaving? Where is she going? With whom?"

"With my grandfather."

"Your grandfather? What's the matter with you? What are you saying?"

"Granny says that Grandpa is coming to take her today, and Mom's weeping. I don't understand what's happening."

My father sighed and said out loud, "All power and might belong to God." Then, he raced to my grandmother's room in his pajamas.

My grandmother was sitting beside my mother, whispering to her: "Don't turn off the TV. Don't wear black. Don't cry for me. I'm going to a place where no one mourns. You take this." She reached for a small wooden box. "Here's the money for my burial. I don't like wakes. Recite the Quran for me – just that. This inscribed shawl is all I need. Now, let's fix breakfast."

My parents were dumbfounded when they saw my grandmother energetically prepare breakfast for us, apparently in the best of health, after she had been talking about dying. I didn't understand anything. What had my grandmother been saying about death? Why wasn't my father weeping like my mother?

My father had nothing but tea for breakfast, and my mother could not stop sobbing quietly as she watched my grandmother rush around so alertly that I thought she was counting her steps. As for me, I never left my grandmother's side. I touched her face with both hands. Then, she smiled at me and told me, "Eat. Open your mouth. I will always be with you. Never fear. No matter what happens, I will be near you." Then, she looked at my father and told him, "After the noon prayer, bring a shaykh from the mosque to pray over me and another man to help you carry away my body. I know I'm heavy," she added with a smile.

"Don't say such things. You have a long life ahead of you. This is just a fantasy. Tell me: Did you have a dream?"

"No, but when did you stop paying attention to signs? He promised to come for me during the noon prayer today. Don't you believe me?"

"I don't want to believe this. Please be reasonable."

"I'm not afraid for myself but am concerned about your wife and my young darling – about how they will react."

"I'm not going anywhere today, and God willing nothing bad will happen to you."

I braced myself and pressed up against my grandmother. I whispered to her, "I never want you to leave. I shan't let anything separate us, Granny."

"Who said anything about separation? I will be with you whenever you need me."

"I need you now."

"And I'm by your side you now. Get some paper and your pastels, and let's draw."

I got up and fetched pieces of white paper and colored pastels. I started scribbling, not because I wanted to but for a single reason: to protect my grandmother from death, to keep her from leaving me, to guard myself against the gaping void she would leave when she departed. I ended up drawing a set of black circles along with question marks that represented issues I did not understand. Since we are fated to die, why are we born? Why do we meet, if we are destined to separate? What is death? What are its harbingers?

I started to study my grandmother's face, but it did not look at all different. Her face was as rosy as ever. Moreover, my grandmother hadn't lost any of her faculties or her usual liveliness.

At noon, my grandmother performed her ablutions, donned the white gown she had pulled from the chest, and spread her prayer mat on the floor. Once the call to prayer had reverberated, she began to pray. When she had completed the prayer ritual, she pronounced the Muslim credo, the *shahada*, in a loud voice, and said "Allahu Akbar" three times. Then, she gazed at me with a luminous expression and a smile I had never seen before. She told me, "Your grandfather has come now with my parents to carry me away with them. I entrust you to God's care, which is never lost." Then, she fell face down to the floor.

A Butterfly's Voice

Chapter

7

A Butterfly's Voice

When a stately looking young man with bulging muscles and a Greek nose entered our house, the sensation I experienced was new to me. He looked at me when I was trying to extract myself from the stupor that had overwhelmed me on the unexpected loss of my grandmother. I was feeling a mixture of shock and sorrow then.

I stood at the door to the room where women mourners who had come to console us were forming a row. Some of them surrounded my mother and wept with her while others were adjusting the position of my grandmother's body so her head would lie in the direction of the *Qibla*[16].

When the young man entered, he looked at me as if he had come searching for me. My mournful wail died out in my throat, and I began to weep quietly. Whenever I tried to look at my grandmother's body, which lay before me, my eyes failed me, and I glanced at him instead.

I wanted him to shelter me from my massive grief and my fear of what would happen to me, now that my grandmother had left. But he carefully executed the task entrusted to him and carried her corpse from the room, assisted by my father and two other men.

The moment her body left the room, my link to everyone else was severed too, and I felt overwhelmed by questions I could not answer. *What do I do now? Who will help me bear the massive weight of my sorrow? What is God's relation to me now? Why did He take her from me?*

I left all those women who had crammed into our house and didn't search for my mother and her scalding tears. I could not visualize what my father was doing with the men who had gone off with my grandmother's corpse or what would become of it, because I was – simply put – not only sad but scared. Everything terrified me.

---

[16] Qibla: The direction of the sacred building, the Kaaba at Mecca, to which Muslims turn at prayer.

I quickly ran to find the radio, my grandmother's old radio, and carried it to the roof terrace. I searched the airwaves for a voice that reminded me of my grandmother's but all I could find was a Quran reciter chanting the Throne Verse. [17] I surrendered to his mellow voice and allowed my tears to flow in torrents.

Many grief-filled days, which were characterized by constant weeping and a total loss of any taste for life, followed. I woke to nothingness and fell asleep with it. This time, my grandmother wasn't as good as her word; I did not feel her near me, even though she had promised. Whenever I shouted to summon her, there was no response.

Her bed and my life felt very cold and miserable. My father started to go to work again, and my mother became sadder and sicker.

Attending school became a daily chore I didn't desire to perform at all, but otherwise my life was absurdly ordinary. In the mornings, I woke up in time to head to school and returned at noon without experiencing anything new. I read to escape from my loneliness and anxiety.

Success and excellent performance were expressions that lost their beautiful resonance after my grandmother departed. Day by day and month by month, I found myself ever more apathetic and felt no hope, delight, glee, or any other emotion.

The war's first year ended with a lot of yelling – by the TV presenters who attempted to convince us of some phony victory, by women trailing funeral processions of victims from the battle fronts, and by cheerleaders who futilely tried to raise the morale of soldiers who had no more idea what the point of the war was than we – I mean me and my mother – did.

For his part, my father made a good-faith effort to believe the news that was broadcast endlessly on TV. He would seize any excuse, however slight, to discuss the war with my

---

[17] Quran, 2:255

mother, not because he loved the war or wanted to wade into its specifics but simply to stir her from her silence.

My parents weren't concerned about my academic progress, which I summarized as excellent whenever they inquired, primarily because they were anxious about everyone's fate in this war, about which its masterminds had lied when they claimed it would last ten days.

I didn't realize that Iraq had two armies – the regular one and a "People's Army" – till I saw my father return one day, at noon, carrying a cloth backpack. He entered our house silently and hid the bag behind his bed until evening, when he brought it out and started to try on the military uniform inside it. When my mother saw him don a military belt, boots, and a beret without any word of explanation, she was horrified. She couldn't believe that he too would leave us. She suddenly began to throw up.

Vomit quickly covered the entire area where she sat. My father and I hurried to lift her by her armpits and rush her to the bathroom, where he began to wash her face. Then, I scurried to where she had sat and started cleaning up with a damp, soapy cloth. When my father brought her back to the bedroom, I changed her dirty clothes and then prepared a hot lemon drink for her.

My mother swallowed the brew in little gulps while staring with hatred and disgust at the backpack and its khaki contents. My father was forced to remove his military uniform, which still had some of my mother's vomit on it. He stuffed the clothes in the bag without cleaning the puke off, and then tossed the backpack aside.

Only then did I grasp how much my parents hated that damn war, which was not even worth cleaning puke off a uniform. If it weren't bad enough that the war made me see red, now it also made me smell vomit whenever the television host peered from the screen to try to convince us, fraudulently, that the war would end in victory. Even the patriotic songs and anthems broadcast nonstop on television inspired that stench.

Our days revolved endlessly around some unknown pivot. Everything seemed a blur to me, including the expressions of the people around me. They suggested only fear of the future. I was alarmed by the prospects for me and my mother once my father died as a martyr in this war, especially now that he had started military training with the People's Army.

I brooded at times about whether my mother would die of sorrow and grief when my father died. Given her weak heart, could she be as resilient as she had been when my little brother and grandmother had died? If she died, what would become of me?

For us Iraqis back then, divination wasn't possible, not even for the *jinni*[18] among us.

One week, I pretended to be sick and missed a full week of school, convinced that an Iranian rocket would destroy our house, like many houses in Basra. Then, at least, I could stop brooding about my future, since I would be dead. My plan failed, however, because the war kept on harvesting soldiers and cities near the front, without its rockets having reached my city yet.

I considered suicide but abandoned that idea. If I died, that would leave my ailing mother alone when my father was gone and could not help her. Even if she found someone to assist her, if I died by my own hand, how could I see my grandmother in heaven? She had informed me once that people who commit suicide inevitably land in hell's fire. It was difficult for a girl like me to find a proper way to die. So, I was forced to persevere with my living death, like everyone around me, and not complain.

One day, I left for the teacher training institute as usual, carrying my schoolbag, and walked quickly past a young man who was

---

[18] Jinni: "In Arabic mythology, a supernatural spirit below the level of angels and devils (Encyclopedia Britannica)."

leaning against the wall of the institute. I couldn't figure out why he looked familiar.

I went inside the institute, and the school day continued uneventfully till one p.m., when as usual, I placed the strap for my bag over my shoulder, beneath my abaya, and left with the other departing students, heading home. Then, a short way from the door of the institute, I found him standing with a foot propped against the wall, just as I had seen him that morning. I was shocked to see him smile at me.

I glanced right and left and saw a number of female students nearby. So, I quickened my pace and crammed myself in among them. Then, I almost ran all the way home.

The moment I set foot in our house, I tried to stop thinking about that smiling young man who had waited for me, but his image dominated my imagination. As I ate lunch with my parents, I wondered why he had smiled at me. Did he know me?

Just before I finished eating, I realized I did know him. Yes, I actually knew who he was. I had seen him before, in our house. He had carried away my grandmother's corpse, together with my father and those other men. But the same question still troubled me: why did he smile at me? What did he want from me?

What a brash guy! Could he possibly have stood there all day long, waiting for me to leave the institute, just to smile at me? I didn't believe it. Only a crazy person would do something like that. No, it was inconceivable that he had wasted all those hours waiting for me. No, that was out of the question. Once I finished my homework, I fell asleep.

"Open your eyes, Darling. Why haven't you told me what happened today?"

"Nothing happened, Granny. Nothing at all."

"Really? Nothing happened? Are you sure?"

"Actually . . . something did happen, Granny. Some guy smiled at me today, and that made me angry. It made me feel I'm a flirt whose forehead proclaims she is so 'easy' that any guy may smile at her."

"Who told you about such things?"

"I've read in novels that a man can recognize an easy girl and will make advances toward her."

"Then what?"

"Then, the evil mushrooms."

"You are really a good girl with all these reservations you have. Doesn't a man ever smile at a good girl?"

"I don't know. I haven't read about that."

"Reading's not the only way a person learns, Darling."

"What do you mean, Granny?"

"I mean: why not think that this young man likes or loves you?"

"Are you sure, Granny?"

"Have I ever lied to you?"

Then, my grandmother offered me a white rose, which I accepted and pressed to my chest.

"Wake up! You'll be late for school!"

When I opened my eyes, I found my mother standing beside my bed. She added, "You're smiling. You must have dreamt something lovely."

"Yes, I dreamt about Granny."

The moment I opened the door of our house, preparing to leave, I found him on the sidewalk across the street, holding a flower just like the one my grandmother had given me in my dream. I closed the door quickly behind me so my mother wouldn't see him, and hurried away.

I did not look his way but listened attentively for his footsteps to make sure that he was following me. I became distracted, though, when a group of other students heading to the institute approached me. Each one asked me a question, taking turns:

"Were you running?"

"Why are you panting?"

"Has some passerby upset you?"

"I thought I was late for school. You know I don't like to be tardy."

"Well, you're not late."

"Praise God," I said, feeling relieved.

He wasn't waiting for me when I left school that day, but his image was etched in my mind. I actually imagined he was walking beside me with a steady stride all the way to our house. Even when I helped my mother wash the dishes, it was as if he was standing in a corner of our kitchen, smiling at me. I smiled back at him, too.

Once sleep caressed my eyelids, he visited me in a dream and offered me his rose.

I woke up early the next morning, hoping to see him, but that wish wasn't fulfilled. A sad void lay beyond the door of our house, and its whirlpool swept me away in its bitterness. I surrendered to it without any resistance.

My school day was marred by feelings of annoyance and sadness. I walked slowly home from the institute, and for the first time, my school bag felt heavy on my shoulder. Beneath my abaya, it resembled the large hump of the old woman I had suddenly become.

I cursed the six daily classes that I had to attend, the long hours I spent in school, and the heavy books and notebooks I carried in that bag. I wished the street would become a river so I could toss my bag into it and rest.

I had no explanation for what was happening to me that day and didn't know why all these different feelings were boiling inside me. I couldn't come up with any reason for my intense anger or the annoyance that filled me then.

My feet dragged my body down the street, taking me home. The distance between the institute and our house seemed much longer than usual. My irritability must have obscured my perceptions.

I would have liked it, if a fellow student had walked a part of the way home with me. Then, the two of us could have discussed anything and everything. We would certainly have discussed our teachers, their clothes, which were no longer color-coordinated thanks to the war, and their faces, which showed their fear and anxiety.

We might have talked about the students' constant anger. We might have pondered over the fluctuating schedule of classes or the ever-changing dates of the "regular" monthly exam dates. I was in urgent need of any conversation, no matter how superficial or brief. It would have helped me traverse what now seemed a long or even endless route.

As these notions clashed in my head, I reached the end of our street. I had been feeling sad, irritable, mournful, and angry all day long. But then, I caught sight of his silhouette, standing just where he had been before. I couldn't believe my eyes, and froze in place. Was I actually alone with him now? Or was I seeing a phantom, a mirage?

My heart began to beat really fast and so loudly that I could hear its rhythm when I watched him start to cross the street, heading toward me. I looked right and left to check that the house doors on our street were all closed, terrified that a neighbor might suddenly open one. I quickly ran home.

I had barely reached my hand out to knock on our door, when I heard his soft voice. I stood just where I was, unable to move, like some human statue that had just been brought to life by a magic word.

His eyes caught me off guard, and I returned his look. He smiled at me and gestured to something near me. I looked in that direction but didn't see anything. I glanced back at him and saw him point in the same direction very determinedly. This time, he was smiling broadly. I turned to check that the street was still empty of passersby before I looked where he was pointing – a crack in the wall between our home and our neighbors' house. Scrutinizing that crevice, I spotted an aluminum paper protruding from it. Before I picked it up, I gazed at him again to make sure this was what he meant. He nodded as if he had read my thoughts. So, I quickly pulled out that shiny paper, and saw that some words were written on it. I held it firmly in my right fist, and then moved it to my left hand with an obvious uneasiness.

After I knocked on our door, my mother opened it and found me staring straight into her eyes. I was trying to determine if there was the slightest reflection in them of the young man standing in the street behind me.

"What's the matter with you?" my mother asked. "Why are you staring at me this way?"

"It's nothing."

I walked in and immediately shut the door. I would really have liked to come up with an excuse to open the door and see if he was still standing there.

I was afraid to unclench my hand. Perhaps, there was nothing there. It might be empty. The recent sequence of events might have been nothing but figments of my imagination. I eventually got a hold of myself, and opened my fist. The paper really was there. I opened my book bag, shoved the note into it, and then emerged with an empty hand.

My delight was spoiled by my anxiety about my bag, which now contained my secret. Where should I hide this bag? What if my mother opened it, found the piece of paper, and gave it to my father to read? But what was actually written on it? Why didn't I want to read it now? Was I afraid to read it?

I decided to ignore these questions and let myself feel giddy for the remainder of the day. Once evening came, I would share the secretive note with my grandmother's spirit.

A Butterfly's Voice

Chapter

8

A Butterfly's Voice

For ten mornings in a row, whenever I went out, I found a present stuffed into that crack in the same wall. I always looked right and left to make sure no one was watching. Then, I would pull the present out quickly, put it into my schoolbag, and rush off to school, in a racing pace, dreaming as my wide-open eyes flooded with tears of delight in response to the message.

With that note in my bag, I could not leave the classroom during breaks for fear that one of the mischievous students would look in my bag – as they did with other students, and thus, discover my secret.

Each slip of paper from him contained a message that made my spirit hum. I cried and smiled while reading his notes, and felt a strong desire to shout them out loud. I wanted everyone to know I wasn't a child anymore. Over the last ten days, I had become an adult.

I was a woman in love and loved, a woman with a secret. A man was now escorting her to a territory she had never ventured before. I frequently was forced to restrain myself from dancing with delight to a silent song as I hugged my bag and dozed off in the classroom.

On the eleventh morning, I closed my eyes and reached for the paper in the wall crack, as I did each day after leaving my house, imagining what phrase I would find, and what its form, flavor, scent, and effect on my spirit would be. Would I start weeping or just smile? Would it transport me as far away as the stars or place me on a rose-colored cloud to sing about a reunion with my true love?

I stretched out my hand, but found it enveloped in a frightening void, which crept out of the hole, grabbed my fingers, and pushed them away. I searched that crevice repeatedly but found nothing. Then, I opened my eyes to face a black hole that was preventing me from obtaining my daily share of delight via a present from an unknown young man whom destiny had chosen as my lover.

Where is it? I wondered repeatedly as I searched for it on the ground. *Perhaps, it fell without him noticing when he tried to slip it into the crack*. My anxiety became even more acute when I realized that someone might have seen it, taken it, and even have kept it to use against me.

A scenario quickly took shape in my head. The plot was that a child had found the paper and shown it to his mom, who had read it and found my name on it. She would inevitably tell my parents about their daughter's offense.

I began to tremble fearfully as I pondered how my day would end. Should I go to school or stay home to wait for some woman to knock on the door and spill my secret to my parents?

If I went home now, what would I tell my mother? How could I explain why I was skipping school today? My mind and body were working in a conflicting manner; the faster my thoughts rushed forward, sketching what would happen to me, the more firmly my feet were planted on the earth, refusing to budge. Such a sense of total paralysis afflicted my body that I feared I would slump to the ground.

The neighbor woman opened her door and remarked with a strange smirk I had never seen before, "Good morning. It seems you're going to be late for school today. It's almost eight."

"Morning, Auntie," I replied in a shaky voice. "I must hurry. Yes, I got up late today."

With great effort, I made myself walk away, lifting heavy legs, like a woodsman picking up a heavy load of firewood. Then, with quick steps I raced to the school door, which the workers were about to close. One of the men, though, took pity on me and waited to shut it until after I got in.

I thanked him, gasping for breath, and carried tons of fear with me inside. I was afraid of everything – of being late, of having lost the note, of my neighbor's questionable smile, and so on and so forth.

Once I was seated in the classroom, my thoughts began to rattle around in my head as a whirlwind of questions multiplied there. Did the woman next door know my secret? Had she kept it to show my parents? What did her smirk imply? Did she want to tell me: "I've discovered your secret"?

I would definitely find my mother waiting to vent her anger, grief, and disappointment. I deserved whatever she would do to me today. Why hadn't I told her everything from the beginning? But how would I have dared tell her? I would have been too embarrassed. If my grandmother really had been with me, everything would have been different!

My God, what shall I do now? My teachers sensed that I was nervous but none of them asked me why.

At the end of the school day, a student asked me, "How's your father?"

"He's fine."

"Will he be sent to the front lines?"

"Yes, he will."

"Ah, now I understand why you've seemed so anxious and fearful today. My father's also at the front; my mother says he will return safe and sound."

"Yes, God willing."

I felt like crying but quickly swallowed the tears that were about to trickle down my cheek. I asked myself: *Why are you crying?* Then, I pulled myself together and hurried out the school door without saying goodbye to any of my classmates.

I returned home even faster than I had sped to school that morning. I scrutinized the crevice in the wall but found only a dark pit that virtually screamed emptiness.

I knocked on our house door. My mother opened it but didn't look at me, because she was preoccupied with something. I assumed she was brooding about my secret.

I told myself: *Our neighbor definitely visited my mother this morning and revealed the secretive note. What do I do now?*

I greeted my mother, who returned my greeting coldly. She returned to the kitchen without asking what had happened at school – something she did every day.

Everything in our house was calm – except for me. The hours passed very slowly as I waited for any sign from my mother that someone had spilled my secret to her. Once night fell, a heavy fatigue overwhelmed my body at once and carried me off to sleep. The moment I closed my eyes, my grandmother appeared, and I raced to her for protection. First, she held me to her breast. Then, she lay down with me tenderly, and I felt her warmth surrounding me. So, I started to tell her my story.

I informed her that the daily gift I had come to depend on over the last ten days had gone missing and that my secret might have been revealed to my mother. Just as soon as I had concluded my confession, she gently put her hand on my head and mumbled some words. The only part I grasped was the phrase: "I ask God to protect you from the one coming." Or, had she said, "From what is coming"?

I woke, trembling with fear, and wondered what or who my grandmother's warning referred to.

It took me a full week to calm down after the incident of the missing note, even though I learned from my mother that no neighbor had called on her. My grandmother's words, however, stuck in my mind. I heard them echo there, at times in such a frightening way that I trembled when I was alone, if only briefly.

What was scary about this was that my grandmother had always been forthright with me for my entire life. Who or what was she warning me against? The war which would consume my father? The perpetual darkness of the orphan-hood that would befall me on the death of my mother, who had been ill and grieving since my little brother died? Who? What?

Three months elapsed without me finding another aluminum paper. The crack in the wall had become a hungry, gaping mouth, an empty void as eager as my hand to touch another note.

Then, suddenly, I thought I had deciphered my grandmother's warning. She feared that a handsome, young, insincere lover would captivate me with his lies, that he would pick me from among all the other girls, having decided to capture my heart with his beautiful words only to dump me, laugh at me, mock me – oblivious to the harm he would inflict upon me.

Now, I no longer wanted to see him. Even if he came to apologize and kissed the dirt under my feet, I still wouldn't forgive him for what he had done to me. As long as I lived, I would never forgive him for toying with my virgin emotions. Yet, he wasn't the only person worthy of chastising. How could I have allowed myself to believe him? How could I have let my heart give in to the magic of his words? I wondered just how many other girls he had enchanted with his charm till they stayed awake at night, praying to God to find notes in the walls of their house.

Granny, I beg you to pray for me and lighten the burden of my anger. With your prayers, grant me enough tranquility and calm so I can return to my books, dreams, peace, and solitude.

But, how could I regain my bearings when I lacked his fragrant word to tattoo my mornings with gold? Was that even conceivable?

I returned from school apathetic, preoccupied by various, conflicting feelings. The first of these was that life is meaningless.

My days consisted of rounds of eating, sleeping, and wakefulness governed by the school bell. Everything was even worse than before, because my father was now serving in the People's Army as a combatant at the front lines.

My mother's sorrow acquired new dimensions, her illness grew more severe, and my role evolved gradually from being a devoted daughter to serving as my mother's personal nurse.

Even though I had always detested the smell of medicine, I memorized the hours when my mother was supposed to take her medications and the required dosage. Without any training, I learned intravenous cannulation and how to jab a needle in her skin, which had rapidly wasted away till her bones protruded at an alarming rate. I learned how to comfort her daily with uplifting words, which neither of us believed, because the doctors said her heart was so weak that not even surgery would help. My father was at the front most of the time, and no one knew when the war would end. The TV host, who filled us with lies every moment, was yet one more factor leading me to forget the great lie called "love," even though I had experienced it for a few days.

The only time I truly smiled was when my father, clad in khaki, returned from any of the various fronts – once it was the north, then Basra, and a third time, from I don't know where. He had come home, and that sufficed. That was all my mother and I needed to feel secure, if only for a few days.

Everything transformed when my father entered our house. My mother's face turned a healthy, rosy color, and I became his little girl once more.

I would kiss him affectionately, and he would laugh as I tried to land my kisses on every part of his face, even on his mustache. I would search through his bag, looking for the present he told me he had brought for me from one of those places the television presenters frequently mentioned. Then, he would say, "You'll always be my little girl, no matter how old you get." At such moments, family-warmth filled my spirit, and I felt calm.

During the nights when my father was home, we stayed up late asking him questions, and he responded with stories that were virtually endless, tales that taught us the true meaning of "war," not what government sources wanted us to hear in the form of patriotic anthems and victory announcements that were never founded. He told us once: "We walked over the blackened corpses of slain soldiers without knowing whether they were our comrades or the enemies."

Whenever my father was home, my mother's condition improved a bit, and she would be able to walk and move around, however slowly.

One day, I was surprised to find my mother dressed all in black. She told me she was going to console a relative whose martyred son's body had been sent back home that day. She asked me to accompany her, and I donned the black *thobe* I reserved for Ashura. I didn't refuse, as I was duty-bound to go with her wherever she went because she might require my help, even if my father was with her.

I had never heard of this relative, but her house wasn't very far from ours. We needed to walk only a few blocks for a few minutes. I wondered how close a relative the bereaved woman was. I felt mystified that relatives wouldn't visit each other, not even for family celebrations.

When we neared her street, I could hear people keening. Their wailing was full-throated and thunderous. The entire street seemed to be mourning this martyr.

We recognized his house from the other side of the street by the large cloth banner fastened to the house's façade. Its large, white letters informed us that Ala' Waheed had died a martyr in the Battle of Khorramshahr. Beside the name was a date, which I ignored. On the other side of the house stood a tent that was already packed with male mourners, with even more arriving.

The moment my mother entered the house, she shouted at the top of her lungs, "Yabooo!" as if to inform all the other women that she had arrived. They responded with cries and by slapping their faces and breasts. Soon, my mother's eyes were waterfalls of tears as women took turns beating their breasts restlessly.

I felt sick to my stomach, and a sense of panic began to slowly infiltrate my spirit. This mysterious discomfort had a sharp, bitter taste; I had only experienced it once before – when my grandmother left us, and I feared it. This disturbance swelled inside me till it became a storm that rose to my head, which felt as if it were being blown apart.

So many women were shoving each other, having crowded the confined space where the air was suffocating that I could hardly breathe. I tried to brace myself to stay inside but failed. I left, and once outside, I leaned against the wall. I began to hyperventilate, totally oblivious to the presence of the men who had filled that street or to the looks some guys directed at me. All I wanted was a little air.

A loud wailing drew me back into the house, where I bumped into the visitors who encircled a woman. She was repeatedly screaming, "My son!" as she was pointing toward a large portrait inside a black picture frame.

I lost my balance and fainted when I saw my beloved's face, framed in black, gazing at me, smiling.

A Butterfly's Voice

epilogue

about the Author

A 2018 Pulitzer Poetry Prize nominee and Inner Child Press International Cultural Ambassador to Iraq, Faleeha Hassan is a poet, teacher, editor, writer, and playwright born in Najaf, Iraq in 1967, who now lives in the United States. She is the first woman to write poetry for children in Iraq.

The author has earned her Master's Degree in Arabic Literature and has published twenty-four books. Her poems have been translated into English, Turkmeni, Bosevih, Hindu, French, Italian, German, Kurdish, Spanish, Korean, Greek, Serbian, Albanian, Pakistani, Malayalam and ODIA. She has received many awards in Iraq and throughout the Middle East for her poetry and short stories. A large number of Faleeha Hassan's poems and short stories have appeared in various U.S.-based magazines and literary platforms.

Email: d.fh88@yahoo.com
www.oprah.com/inspiration/faleeha-hassan-poet-and-writer

about the $\mathcal{T}$ranslator

William Hutchins, who is based in North Carolina, has received his education at Berea, Yale, and the University of Chicago. He has been awarded the National Endowment for the Arts grant for literary translation twice; first, in 2005-2006 for his translation of *The Seven Veils of Seth* by the Libyan Tuareg author, Ibrahim al-Koni (Garnet Publishing), and again in 2011-2012, for al-Koni's novel *New Waw*. Literary translations by Hutchins have appeared in Words Without Borders, Banipal Magazine of Modern Arab Literature and InTranslation.

The translation work William Hutchins has completed for Arabic novels include *Palace Walk*, *Palace of Desire*, *Sugar Street*, and *Cairo Modern* by the Nobel Laureate Naguib Mahfouz (Anchor Books); *Basrayatha* by the Iraqi author Muhammad Khudayyir (Verso); *The Last of the Angels* (The Free Press), *Cell Block 5* (Arabia Books), and *The Traveler and the Innkeeper* (American University in Cairo Press) by the Iraqi author Fadhil al-Azzawi; *Return to Dar al-Basha* by the Tunisian author Hassan Nasr (Syracuse), and *Anubis* (The American University in Cairo Press) and *Puppet* (Texas) by Ibrahim al-Koni. Literary translations by Hutchins released within the period of one year alone include *The Diesel* by Thani al-Suwaidi (ANTIBOOKCLUB); *Return of the Spirit* by Tawfiq al-Hakim (revised edition, Lynne Rienner Publishers); *The Grub Hunter* by Amir Tag Elsir (Pearson: African Writers Series), and *A Land Without Jasmine* by Wajdi al-Ahdal (Garnet).

The Author's

Accomplishments

Books in English

Breakfast for Butterflies. Inner Child Press, Ltd.
May 3, 2018

Mass Graves. Inner Child Press, Ltd.
July 10, 2017

We Grew up at the Speed of War. Lulu.com.
January 13, 2016

Lipstick. Transcendent Zero Press.
December 3, 2016

Awards and Prizes

Pushcart Prize Nomination, 2019

Pushcart Prize Nomination, 2018

Pulitzer Poetry Prize Nomination, 2018

Srbrun Poveilu / Silver Medal from the Mesopotamia
Cultural Center, Belgrade–Serbia, 2018

The Najafi Creative Festival for Poetry, 2012

The Shaheed al-Mihrab Foundation Prize for Short
Story

The Prize of al-Mu'temar for Poetry, 2010

Phoenix International Festival of Arts and Culture,
2010

The Naziq al-Malaika Prize, 2008

World Association of Arab Translators and Linguists
(WATA)

Literary Contributions

(Journals and Magazines)

Philadelphia Poets 22
Harbinger Asylum
Brooklyn Rail
Screamin Mamas
The Galway Review
Words Without Borders
TXTOBJX
InTranslation
SJ Magazine
NonDoc
Wordgathering
Scarlet Leaf Review
Courier-Post
I am not a silent poet
Taos Journal of Poetry and Art
Inner Child Magazine
Atlantic City Magazine
The Guardian
Life and Legends
Indiana Voice Journal
The Bees Are Dead
IWA
Poetry Soup
Adelaide Literary Magazine

Philly
The Fountain Magazine
Dryland: Los Angeles Underground Art & Writing
The Blue Mountain Review
Setu Monthly
OTOLITHS
DODGING THE RAIN
American Poetry Review
Uljana Wolf Journal
ARCS Journal
Tiferet and Ice Cream Poetry Anthology
Opa Anthology of Contemporary Women's Poetry
Bacopa Literary Review
Better Than Starbucks Poetry Magazine
Tweymatikh ZQH Magazine
Tuck Magazine
Street Light Press
Empty Mirror
Spider Mirror Journal
Turn a Page or Two within Darkness and Light Journal
RAMINGO
Pyrokinection
Anapest
New Myths
The Oprah Magazine
Paragon Press
Sixfold Fiction and Poetry
Our Poetry Archive

L3 Magazine
Ethos Literary Journal
WHERE WORDS MATTER Spillwords Press
Magnum Opus: A Poetry Anthology on Universal
       Oneness
Alien Buddha Press
Mama's Smile
The Love Poems Anthology
First Class Literary Magazine
The U.S. World War I Centennial Commission
Living Peace: Peace Poetry Anthology
Bacopa Literary Review
Consequence Magazine
Philadelphia Poets Journal
'We Got This' Journal
Lift Every Voice: An Anthology of Poetry

*F*aleeha *H*assan's

Web Links

Web Site
www.faleehahassan.com

FaceBook
www.facebook.com/profile.php?id=100
004321951511

Instagram
www.instagram.com/faleeha_hassan

Twitter
twitter.com/fh88d?lang=en

Inner Child Press International

Inner Child Press International is a publishing company founded and operated by Writers. Our personal publishing experiences provide us an intimate understanding of the sometimes-daunting challenges writers, new and seasoned, may face in the business of publishing and marketing their Creative "Written Work".

For more Information:

Inner Child Press International

www.innerchildpress.com

intouch@innerchildpress.com

'building bridges of cultural understanding'

www.innerchildpress.com

www.ingramcontent.com/pod-product-compliance
Lightning Source LLC
Chambersburg PA
CBHW030147200626
46812CB00015B/1737